TreeTops
Myths and Legends

Mythical Beasts and Fabulous Monsters

Timothy Knapman

OXFORD

OXFORD
UNIVERSITY PRESS

Great Clarendon Street, Oxford, OX2 6DP,
United Kingdom

Oxford University Press is a department of the University of Oxford.
It furthers the University's objective of excellence in research, scholarship,
and education by publishing worldwide. Oxford is a registered trade mark
of Oxford University Press in the UK and in certain other countries

© Timothy Knapman 2010

The moral rights of the author have been asserted

First published 2010

This edition published 2014

British Library Cataloguing in Publication Data
Data available

978-0-19-844638-5

5 7 9 10 8 6

Paper used in the production of this book is a natural, recyclable product
made from wood grown in sustainable forests. The manufacturing process
conforms to the environmental regulations of the country of origin.

Printed in China by Leo Paper Products Ltd.

Acknowledgements
Cover illustrated by Andrés Martínez Ricci
Inside illustrations by Mike Phillips, Harris Sofokleous,
Andrés Martínez Ricci and Lily Trotter

Book quiz answers
1 a
2 *The Feathers in the Flames*
3 Change the black sails for white ones, so
his father would know he was alive.

Now I'm sure you've heard of Athens. It's the most beautiful city on the Greek mainland. The most beautiful city in the world, if you ask me. You can probably guess that it's named after Athena, the goddess of wisdom. So, naturally, those of us who live there are pretty brainy.

Which is more than you can say for those people who live out on the Greek islands.

Don't get me wrong. I'm not a snob. I just think being stuck in the middle of the sea on a godforsaken rock covered in sheep is bound to send you stark raving mad sooner or later.

Take the poor souls that live on Crete! I mean, okay so they've got a few decent beaches, but have you heard the story about their queen?

No?

It's very weird.

What happened was this. Minos, who is the King of Crete, had promised that every year he'd sacrifice his best bulls to Poseidon, the god of the sea.

That all went very well until one year Minos

• *Athena:* (say) 'uh-thee-nuh'.   • *Minos:* (say) 'my-noss'.
• *Poseiden:* (say) 'puh-sy-dun'.

had this especially fine bull. Bright eyes, glossy coat, horns as sharp as two short stabbing swords ... the works.

The idea of giving up this fantastic bull for slaughter, just to appease some watery twerp who gets his earholes scraped for barnacles twice a year, was too much for Minos.

So he broke his promise and hid the bull from Poseidon's priests.

Bad idea.

This is the gods we're talking about, after all, and our Greek gods aren't like some. They're not a bunch of bearded, sandal-wearing hippies droning on about peace, love and understanding. Oh no.

They're a bunch of bearded, sandal-wearing psychos who can't wait for you to get on the wrong side of them so they can do something really nasty to you.

Of course Poseidon found out. And of course he was furious. And of course the only thing he could think of was how to get his own back on this puny human who had dared to defy him!

'So this bull is too good for me, is it?' he roared. 'I suppose Minos wants to keep it alive so it can father lots of little bulls. Oh, it'll father a little bull all right!'

GRRRR!

Then he laughed his scariest laugh (like a hurricane that's got the giggles). He had a word with Eros – you know Eros: the little boy with the bow and arrow. All he has to do is shoot you through the heart and you fall madly in love, whether you want to or not.

TWANG!

The next time Minos' wife, Queen Pasiphaë, was passing the meadow where Minos had hidden the bull, guess what?

• *Eros:* (say) 'ee-ross'. • *Pasiphaë:* (say) 'puh-sif-uh-ee'.

She fell madly in love with it!

If that wasn't bad enough, pretty soon she was expecting a baby. I told you this story was weird.

Naturally, Minos was thrilled to hear that his wife was pregnant. He didn't know what Poseidon had done.

You can imagine what it must have been like for him, pacing up and down outside his wife's bedroom, listening out for the first cries of his new-born baby son ...

Only to hear from behind those closed doors ... the sound of mooing!

Minos burst into the bedroom and there it was, cradled in its mother's arms. A baby boy ... with a bull's head and horns, and a little swishy tail.

The Minotaur!

At first, Minos and Pasiphaë tried to carry on as if nothing was wrong. They had to use metal bars on the Minotaur's playpen to stop him getting out and you needed a strong stomach to change his nappy – but it all went well enough for a while.

Then one afternoon, the nanny was giving the little prince a tickle and what did he do?

Did he giggle, did he gurgle, did he spit up a bit of milk, perhaps, like any normal baby?

No.

He ate her.

It wouldn't have been too bad, but a couple of the palace guards got involved, trying to pull the poor woman free, so the Minotaur ate them too.

Kids, eh?

The moment Minos found out he was furious (those guards cost ten drachmas each!). Pasiphaë begged him to be merciful, but Minos was having none of it. He ordered a great architect to build a labyrinth – a maze so complicated that no one could ever find their way out of it – underneath the royal palace.

There he imprisoned the Minotaur.

But he did promise Pasiphaë one thing: her child would never go hungry.

And that's where I come into the story.

11

Chapter 2

You remember how I said that my city, Athens, was named after the goddess of wisdom and that we're all jolly brainy? Well, one thing we're *not* good at is fighting. Certainly not when faced with an army which has been stuck out in the middle of the sea on a godforsaken rock covered in sheep.

Like the Cretans.

That's why, at this particular time, we are part of the empire of King Minos and have to do whatever he says.

So when Minos commanded that we should send seven young men and seven young women to Crete, my father, the King, obeyed. Even though word of the labyrinth and its monstrous inmate had reached him and he knew what fate awaited those fourteen young people.

I couldn't bear the thought of it, and I told my father as much. I had to do something to stop those poor people being eaten alive and I begged him to send me, too.

'But, my son, you'll die!' he wailed.

'Only if I can't think of a way to save us all,' I said. 'If I'm that stupid, I don't deserve to live, never mind call myself an Athenian!'

All night we argued, until eventually he agreed to let me go.

'You must promise me one thing, Theseus,' he said as I was getting ready. 'I could not bear to see your ship come back to harbour only to have some sailor tell me that you are dead ...'

That's it! I remember now!

Ye gods, I can be stupid sometimes!

This is what's so really amazingly important about the black sails!

My dad said that he would give our ship black sails, but that if I killed the Minotaur and came out of the labyrinth alive, I should change those sails for the white ones he put in the hold.

He'll be up on the high cliffs every day, looking out for the return of our ship. If he sees it come back with white sails, he'll know I'm alive and he'll rejoice. If he sees black sails, he'll know I'm dead and he'll hurl himself off those cliffs and join me in the Underworld.

So, note to self: remember to change the black sails for white ones before we get in sight of land. Now, where was I?

Oh yes, so I got on the ship with the other

thirteen Athenians and off we set for Crete. I
have to say that I had a few wobbly moments
on the journey. I mean, I knew I was brave
and brainy and all that, but I was hoping that
some brilliant idea for killing the Minotaur and
getting away with it would pop into my head
before we arrived.

It didn't.

I was still puzzling about it when we reached
Crete and they herded us into this big cage in
the market square. I nearly had something when
someone poked me in the ribs.

'Need any help?' said a voice.

Honestly! People!

'Yes, I need you to go away!' I snapped,
and tried to remember the brilliant plan I was
hatching.

'Want to defeat the Minotaur and escape the
labyrinth?' she went on.

'Well, *dur*!' I looked up.

It was Princess Ariadne, the daughter of
King Minos!

'This is all you need!' she said and she gave me a very useful-looking sword and not-nearly-so-useful-looking ball of thread. 'Hide the sword and tie one end of the thread to your wrist.'

But why on earth was she doing all this for me?

'Once my father learns that I've helped you to kill the Minotaur, I will not be safe here,' she said. 'You must promise to take me back to

Athens with you.'

Of course. I should have guessed. One look at her face, all googly eyed and slack jawed, and you could see that she'd fallen madly in love with a certain recklessly good-looking Athenian prince.

What do you mean, 'Who?'!

Me, of course!

'Yeah, all right,' I said.

It was all I had time for, because just then a bunch of guards grabbed hold of us and bundled us into the labyrinth. Ye gods, it was hot down there – and what a mess!

Don't get me wrong. I'm not the tidiest person in the world, but you'd think with all the spare time he had, the Minotaur could have smartened the place up a bit: cleared away some of the bones, washed the walls. After all, he was expecting guests. Even if he was going to eat them.

As for the smell –!

Really, you don't want to know.

I was looking around for a window to open when we heard it.

The bellowing roar. Echoing around the walls so we had no idea where it had come from. In front of us, behind us.

It seemed to come from everywhere.

Of course I'm incredibly brave and nothing frightens me, but as everyone else was shrieking in terror and running for their lives, I thought I might as well join in. Just to be polite. Around this corner we went, down that corridor, turning left, turning right. Talk about a running buffet! Talk about fast food!

The annoying thing was that no matter how hard we pushed ourselves, the roar of the Minotaur got closer and closer.

Then suddenly we hit it.

A dead end.

It was only when I stopped running that I realised how hard my heart was hammering in my chest.

It was minutes before I had enough breath to speak.

'We'll just have to turn round and go back. Maybe we lost him, maybe ...'

My voice died in my throat.

All my companions were frozen. Their wild eyes fixed on a great shape looming in the darkness at the edge of the torchlight.

He was seven, maybe eight feet tall, and those eyes! Like a lion's – blazing amber. Burning into mine.

'Oh fiddlesticks,' I said. Or something like it.

The Minotaur had started his charge even before I realised. He came straight at me, slamming through the air like a thunderbolt. I had no time to think, I had no time to plan.

There he was, upon me, his great, yellow fanged jaws parting, ready to bite. Honestly, with a couple of rich parents like he had, you'd have

thought he could afford a toothbrush!

Then I felt it: a great shudder of muscle trembling through me. I saw those stupid, animal eyes go blind and I looked down.

Somehow, the sword that Ariadne had given me was in my hand. I had killed him.

Of course, my companions went crazy with relief, but we weren't exactly home and dry. The architect who'd built the labyrinth was a clever fellow. We could be wandering its corridors for years with no chance of ever getting out.

That's when I felt a twitch. Somehow, as we had been running, the ball of thread Ariadne had given me must have come loose, because all I had hold of now was one end of it, tied around my wrist.

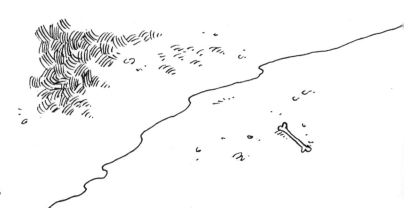

'Of course!' I shouted as I realised what she'd done. 'Oh, you clever, wonderful girl!' I ordered my companions to keep very close to me as I followed the thread out of the dead end, turning left, turning right, up this corridor, around that corner ...

... Until it brought us to daylight and the place where Ariadne was waiting for us, holding the other end.

I'm not ashamed to say I kissed her. I've never been so pleased to see anyone in my life!

Chapter 3

'The moment my father hears of this, we are all dead!' said Ariadne.

I don't know why she was so worried. They're an idle bunch, the Cretans. The harbour was all shuttered up when we reached our boat. They must have been having a lie-in. We were far out to sea before they even knew we were gone.

Now would you do me a favour?

Would you please read back over the last few pages and tell me exactly where I promised Ariadne that I'd marry her?

Take her back to Athens with me, that's what I said.

But the moment we were out of sight of land, she started on. Nagging me about all the things I was going to have to change about myself if I was going to be a fit husband for a princess of Crete!

Don't get me wrong. I was grateful for her help but it wasn't long before she was really getting on my nerves! Just as well we Athenians are brainy, isn't it?

'All this monster killing takes it out of a chap,' I yawned, 'and I've never been able to sleep on a ship. Why don't we pull in to the next island and get a bit of shut-eye so that we'll look our best for our triumphal entry into Athens?'

Ariadne didn't take much persuading; all that nagging would tire anyone out.

She was fast asleep before we'd even pitched camp. I don't want to be rude, by the way, but listening to her snore, you could tell she was the Minotaur's sister!

I don't feel bad about sneaking away and leaving her there all alone. It's a nice enough island. There are plenty of berries and nuts about: she won't starve. Besides, someone's bound to come along and pick her up eventually.

I can see land now. Home. And the high cliffs that look down to the sea.

Wait a minute. There's something I've got to do.

I've completely forgotten what it is again!

Look, though! That little figure you can just about see up there, it's my dad! I'm waving, but I don't think he can see me. These black sails keep getting in the way.

Something really amazingly important or something dreadful is going to happen.

No, it's gone.

I'll have to tell the story again. Yes. That's bound to jog my memory.

The Watcher in the Waves

A story based on Viking myth and legend

Chapter 1

 One year, spring forgot to come to one particular Viking tribe.

The sun did not shine, the snow did not melt, the crops did not grow and the people began to starve.

'My friends!' roared their king, Olaf the Violent, over the rumbling of everyone's empty stomachs. 'I have had a jolly good think about our problem. What we need is a clear, intelligent and sensible plan to get us out of this mess. So, I propose ...'

The King took a deep breath. Everyone leaned forward to hear his wisdom.

'I propose', he continued, 'that we get in our longship and find another tribe of Vikings and bash them over the head!'

'HOORAY!' cheered all the men.

'*WHAT*?' sneered all the women. 'How is THAT going to put food on our tables exactly?'

'Dear ladies,' said King Olaf. He was surprised – and a little hurt – that the women of his tribe hadn't seen how brilliant his idea was. 'That is the Viking answer to every problem!'

'We know!' said the women bitterly.

'Well it's bound to work eventually,' said King Olaf.

The women of the village threw their hands up in despair but the men polished their spiky helmets and sharpened their war axes. They stuck extra nails into their battle hammers and prepared for war.

All the men, that is, except one. He was young and his name was Snorri the Dreamer.

Snorri had never been very keen on fighting. He would much rather have read the great sagas

and watched the sun set. He loved nature and enjoyed going for long walks to explore the fjord and the countryside around the village.

'In other words, he's stupid,' said Halfdan the Unhinged.

'Halfdan, don't be so rude about your brother!' snapped their mother and she smacked Halfdan over the head with a heavy frying pan.

'*Well* ...' said Halfdan, after he'd picked himself up off the floor and stopped screaming. 'We have a noble tradition in this family. We're berserkers, shield-chewers, head-bangers. Since the beginning of time, we've had the special privilege of being first into battle, the first to charge screaming at the enemy –'

'The first to get killed!' said Snorri.

'Exactly!' said Halfdan, with a proud smile. 'As everyone knows, every Viking who dies bravely in battle goes straight to Valhalla where there's food and drink and singing forever and ever.'

'Until ...' said Snorri.

'Until Ragnarok,' said Halfdan. 'The great battle at the end of time, when Good and Evil clash and everything gets destroyed and you get to die bravely all over again. Whoopee! I do hope when I die it's long and messy and *extremely* painful.'

'Look at the world around you, Halfdan,' said Snorri. 'The sea, the sky, the beautiful countryside. Goodness knows we have little enough time to enjoy it already. Why would you want to make your life even shorter?'

Before Halfdan could answer, his mum smacked Snorri over the head with the very heavy frying pan.

'Sorry, Snorri,' she said, 'but your brother's right. We have traditions in this family.'

• *Valhalla:* (say) 'val-ha-luh'.   • *Ragnarok:* (say) 'rag-nuh-rock'.

Chapter 2

When Snorri woke up, he was sitting in the longship next to his brother. Someone had dressed him up in his battle gear and stuck a sword in his hand.

'AT LAST, HE IS AWAKE! 'OW KIND OF YOU TO JOIN US, YOU WORTHLESS SPAWN OF SNIVELLING SEA SCUM!' bellowed a massive Viking straight into Snorri's face.

'Oh, hello Uncle Eric,' said Snorri. 'How's Auntie Agnetha?'

'STILL MAD, THANKS FOR ASKING!' bellowed Uncle Eric.

'I bet you're excited now, aren't you?' asked Halfdan.

'I've got the worst headache of my life. Uncle Eric's just shouted at me so loudly I think my brain's turned to soup and I'm about to be violently killed,' said Snorri. 'Of course I'm excited.'

'Me too!' said Halfdan. He looked like a little boy waiting for Christmas morning.

'Oh bother!' said Snorri suddenly.

'What's the matter?' said Halfdan.

'Forgotten my pyjamas,' said Snorri.

'This is a Viking raiding party!' said Halfdan. 'You won't be needing your pyjamas!'

'What, go to sleep the night before an important battle without my special jim-jams on?' said Snorri. 'Not likely. I won't get my proper rest. I'll be all grumpy and that'll really take the fun out of being horribly killed. Won't be long!'

Before Halfdan could stop him, Snorri had jumped out of the longship and run off.

Snorri knew that if he went home the Viking warriors would find him and drag him straight back to the ship. So, instead, he followed the steep path up the side of the fjord to his favourite place. He planned to wait there until he saw that the longship was far out to sea.

'You haven't got any special jim-jams!'

Snorri jumped.

'Halfdan! How did you find me?'

'I may be incredibly thick, but I'm not *stupid*!' said Halfdan. 'You're always going on about watching the sun set, and this is the best place to see it for miles around. Now come on, hurry! The King doesn't want to miss the tide!'

'He's not going to,' said Snorri, and he
pointed. Down below them, the longship slipped
out of the fjord and made for the open sea.

'Oh, *what*?!' cried Halfdan. 'Well that's just
brilliant, isn't it? Bang goes my chance to get
horribly killed. I hope you're proud of yourself.
I could have been on the end of someone's sword

by half past three! I could have been in Valhalla in time for tea! So how am I going to get to paradise now, Mr Brainbox?'

'Look around you, Halfdan,' said Snorri. 'You're in paradise already!'

Halfdan had to agree. Even with all the snow and ice everywhere, it was a beautiful spot but he was still very angry.

'In any case,' said Snorri, 'we have a serious problem. There is no food and pretty soon our people are going to start dying. I can't imagine the King's plan is going to do any good so it's up to us to save the tribe.'

'What can we do?' asked Halfdan.

'I've been thinking about that,' said Snorri. 'We can go fishing!'

'How?' said Halfdan.

'We can borrow Canute the Stinky's boat!'

'But it stinks!'

'*Obviously.*'

'And in any case', said Halfdan, 'we're rubbish at fishing!'

'That doesn't matter,' said Snorri. 'I remember reading that the best place to go fishing is in the waters just above where the Kraken lurks. There are always plenty of fish and they swim straight into your nets. It's perfect!'

'Perfect except for one thing,' said Halfdan. 'The Kraken isn't going to let us pinch all those fish. It's a ginormous man-eating sea monster that looks like a gigantic crab!'

'It looks like a gigantic octopus!' said Snorri.

'Crab!'

'Octopus!'

'Crab!'

'Octopus!'

'Does it matter?' said Snorri. 'The important thing is that this plan is dangerous and it's bound to result in almost-certain death!'

'Is it?' said Halfdan. 'Well why didn't you say so before? What are we waiting for?'

Chapter 3

Snorri was right. There were plenty of fish in the waters above the Kraken and they did seem to swim right into the brothers' nets. In no time, their little boat was piled high with enough fish to feed their tribe for a whole year.

'Even better, nobody had to get horribly killed by a gigantic octopus,' said Snorri.

'Crab,' said Halfdan.

'Octopus!' said Snorri.

'Crab!' said Halfdan.

They were so busy arguing that they didn't notice as the waters around them began to bubble. At last, with a great roar, a monster with the tentacles of a gigantic octopus and the shell and claws of a gigantic crab burst out of the sea.

'Well that settles that,' said Snorri. 'We're both right.'

'Afternoon,' said the Kraken. 'I've been watching you two for a while now but I still can't decide ...'

'Decide on what?' asked Halfdan.

'Which one of you I'm going to eat first, of course!' said the Kraken.

Before the brothers knew what was happening, the Kraken had grabbed them in its great tentacles. It swung them high into the air.

'Eany-meany-my-nee-mo,' the Kraken chanted. 'Catch a Viking by his toe. If he squeals, eat him –'

'Hooray!' squealed Halfdan. 'I'm about to die an extremely painful death!'

'Right!' roared the Kraken. 'In you go!'

'Wait!' shouted Snorri just as the Kraken was about to bite Halfdan's head off.

'You're not trying to stop me eating you, I hope,' it said. 'Sailors try all sorts of clever tricks to stop me eating them, but they never work, you know.'

'How could they?' said Snorri. 'You're far too clever to be tricked by silly little sailors!'

'That is a lovely thing to say,' said the Kraken. 'A truly lovely thing to say! What kind of vicious, heartless creature could eat you both up after you've said something as lovely as that?'

The Kraken thought for a moment.

'This one!' it cried. 'I'm starving!'

'I was just thinking that we're going to taste awfully dry,' said Snorri.

'Dry? What are you talking about?' said the Kraken. 'There's water all around us!'

'Yes, but it's salt water,' said Snorri. 'Ugh! It dries out your mouth! No, everyone knows that

a Viking tastes best when washed down with lashings of lovely Rune Juice!'

'Rune Juice?' said the Kraken.

'Yes, it's a Viking brand of fruit juice. My favourite flavour is apple,' said Snorri. 'Though some people prefer blackcurrant. Hey, what a stroke of luck, we're not far from the island of Hlesey, the home of the sea god Aegir! He makes the best Rune Juice in the world, especially for the gods! In his golden hall, there are cups that refill themselves every time you take a drink!'

'But I'm ginormous,' said the Kraken. 'I can't drink out of some measly little cup!'

'You won't have to,' said Snorri. 'Aegir has a cauldron full of Rune Juice that was stolen from the Land of the Giants. It's five miles deep!'

'What are we waiting for?' said the Kraken. He plonked Snorri and Halfdan back down on the deck of their fishing boat and pushed them all the way to Hlesey.

For a long time, Halfdan didn't say anything. He just stared at Snorri. Then at last he said,

'It was all going brilliantly. I was just about to die an extremely painful death. I could have been in Valhalla now if it wasn't for you!'

'It doesn't count,' said Snorri.

'What?' said Halfdan.

'You have to die in battle if you're going to get to Valhalla. Being eaten by a sea monster doesn't count.'

'Even if it's an extremely painful death?'

'Oh look, we're here!'

As Snorri knew most about the gods from all the sagas he'd read, he was the one to knock on the door of Aegir's golden hall.

'Don't think you can walk in there and then sneak out the back and escape,' said the Kraken. 'I'm holding your ship, and your brother, hostage.'

'At last!' snapped Aegir, the sea god, as he opened the great door of his golden hall. 'We thought you'd never get here! Wait a minute, who are you?'

'Greetings, mighty god!' said Snorri, and he

bowed his head. 'I am Snorri, son of Beowulf the Berserker. My friends and I have come to sample some of your famous Rune Juice.'

'Clear off!' cried Aegir. 'I'm too busy. I have to prepare dinner for all the gods of Asgard and the ingredients for my starter still haven't arrived.

Wait till I get my hands on that delivery boy! The only reason I opened the door was that I thought you might be him.'

'Perhaps I can help you,' said Snorri. 'In return for some Rune Juice for me and my companions, I will give you the recipe and the ingredients for a starter worthy of the gods themselves.'

'Really?' said Aegir.

'Yes, I call it Seafood Surprise,' said Snorri. 'If you don't believe me, just look over there.' He pointed to where the Kraken was keeping a close eye on Halfdan and the boat that was piled high with delicious fish.

'The gods do like their seafood,' said Aegir thoughtfully. 'All right, but it had better be a really wonderful recipe!'

Inside his magnificent golden hall, Aegir poured cups of Rune Juice for the two Vikings. Then he helped the Kraken clamber into the vast cauldron.

'Cheers!' said Snorri.

'Cheers!' said Aegir. 'Now come on then,

where's this recipe you promised me? The gods
will be here in a few hours.'

'Of course,' said Snorri. 'Give me a pen and
paper and I shall write it out for you.'

'So you do catering for the gods, eh?' Halfdan asked Aegir. 'Could you settle an argument for me? I want to go to Valhalla. I'm about to die an extremely painful death, but my brother says it doesn't count because I'm going to be eaten by a sea monster, not killed in battle.'

'That reminds me!' roared the Kraken as it wallowed in the cauldron of Rune Juice. 'I'm supposed to be eating you Vikings! Come on, sea god, throw them in and I can have them washed down with mouthfuls of this delicious drink!'

Snorri finished writing the recipe and handed it to Aegir.

'This looks like a real winner,' said Aegir as he read. 'Thank you, young Viking.'

'Now I think we'll be off, Halfdan,' said Snorri. 'Goodbye, Aegir. Goodbye, Kraken.'

'But I'm going to devour you!' bellowed the Kraken.

'Yes, I'm sorry, but I don't think that will be possible, after all,' said Snorri. 'You see, the Seafood Surprise recipe I've just given Aegir is

for Kraken in Rune Juice. It's very tasty by all
accounts. I'm sure the gods will love it!'

'Wait! No!' wailed the Kraken. 'Get me out
of here! Get me out!'

Chapter 4

So Snorri and Halfdan sailed home from the island of Hlesey.

When the women of the tribe saw all the delicious fish piled high on their boat, they cheered and set about cooking a sumptuous feast.

They were about to sit down to eat when the King and the Viking warriors returned. They looked exhausted and weak from lack of food.

'We didn't find anyone to bash on the head,' said King Olaf, quietly. 'The lads weren't exactly

a hundred per cent, not having eaten anything for so long, so we couldn't row far. Then it got dark and we were all a bit ... frightened. So we thought we'd best just come home.'

'Well there's plenty of food here now,' said Snorri. 'Welcome back!'

There was much feasting that night, and dancing and drinking to the health of Snorri and Halfdan, the two great heroes of the tribe.

'Maybe there *is* more to life than a horribly painful death,' said Halfdan as he took a great

drink of Rune Juice. 'Thank you, brother, for saving me!'

He and Snorri embraced.

By the firelight, they watched as Viking warriors hugged the wives and children they hadn't expected ever to see again.

'Yes,' said Snorri. 'There's a lot to be said for being alive!'

The Sailor in the Sky

A folk tale from the Middle East

Chapter 1

Sinbad grew up in the port of Basra. Seeing all the ships coming and going with their cargoes of jewels and spices, fine silks and exotic animals, he couldn't wait until he was old enough to go to sea himself. He wanted to become a hero and have adventures.

His father tried to stop him, of course.

'Adventures?' he laughed when Sinbad told him about his hopes and dreams. 'What nonsense! A good job with the family business, that's what you want my boy!'

Sinbad couldn't believe his ears. Stay in dull old Basra all his life, with his nose buried in a dusty accounts book until he went blind with boredom? Not likely!

Then Sinbad's father did something even more thoughtless. He dropped dead, leaving Sinbad all his money. Suddenly, Sinbad was so fabulously wealthy that he never had to do a day's work for the rest of his life.

What a disaster!

'A hero is supposed to start with nothing,' thought Sinbad. 'It says so in all the story books. He has to go out into the world to seek his fortune. Why would a hero risk his life travelling to dangerous places in leaky old ships if he'd just been given a fortune? It's no good: I shall have to lose all my money.'

I don't know if you've ever tried to lose an enormous amount of money, but it's not as easy as it sounds.

You can't just leave it on a park bench (Sinbad tried that), there's far too much of it. Someone on a passing camel is bound to notice and say, 'Excuse me, young man. I do believe you've just left an enormous amount of money on that park bench!'

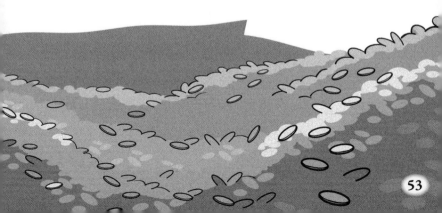

No, you have to really work at it. You have to spend it on lots of things that are very expensive and that break the moment you get them home. You have to lend it to an awful lot of people who are very forgetful and never pay you back. You have to invite all the town's greedy guts to dinner over and over again and hope that they will eat you out of house and home.

It takes *ages*!

There were times when Sinbad thought he was working far harder to lose his father's money than the old man had ever worked to earn it!

At last, though, it was gone. He had lost everything. He didn't have a single penny to his name.

'Thank goodness,' thought Sinbad. 'Now I can become a hero!'

He went straight to the docks and got a job on the next boat out.

Chapter 2

Sinbad found work on a merchant vessel that sailed from port to port, from island to island. Everyone on board talked about the great fortune they were certain to collect on their voyage, though funnily enough they never seemed to buy or sell anything.

Not that Sinbad minded. He was Sinbad the Sailor at last. He'd left Basra far behind and every day there were new and exciting things to see.

It wasn't long, though, before he grew restless. Sinbad was hungry for adventure, but he never once saw a pirate, or a sea monster or even a beautiful young woman singing strange songs to lure his ship onto the rocks.

So he decided to liven things up a bit.

One dinner time, he put salt in the sugar bowl and sugar in the salt cellar, just to see the looks on his shipmates' faces. He smeared the deck with soap so that people would trip over and fall

into the sea. He even set fire to one man's beard.

It was terrific fun!

All right, so Sinbad was the only person who ever actually *laughed*, but he was sure that, in their own stern and grumpy way, the rest of the crew were enjoying it too.

Until, that was, he woke up one morning to find they'd left him behind on an island in the middle of nowhere.

They'd told him they were just going to camp on the island overnight. They promised to wake him up before they left. 'We won't abandon you here so that you have to live out the rest of your days on this miserable rock all alone,' they said. 'That would be a *bad sin*!'

Sinbad didn't think it was much of a joke, but he laughed along with everyone else, just to be friendly.

Well so much for friendliness!

Come to think of it, if he was stuck on this island for the rest of his life, how was he ever going to become a hero?

There was nothing for it. Sinbad would have to find some way to escape.

He climbed to the top of a tall tree.

First, he looked west, but all he could see were miles and miles of empty ocean, stretching away to the far horizon. There was no way he was going to swim home and, no matter how hard he squinted, he couldn't see any sign of a passing ship that might rescue him.

So he turned and looked east, across the island. About a mile in front of him, a great wall of jagged rocks rose up into the clouds. There was no way he was ever going to get past that!

'Oh well, that's *brilliant*, isn't it?' cried Sinbad.

He was trapped! Doomed! Done for!

He was just about to give up the ghost, and go stark staring potty, when he caught sight of something strange on a ledge halfway up that wall of jagged rocks. The something strange looked round and white. It was so odd, Sinbad decided to go and investigate. 'After all,' he thought, 'what have I got to lose?'

It took him the best part of the day to reach that ledge. He was sweaty and breathless from the climb but still his heart skipped a beat when he saw that the round and white something was an egg. No ordinary egg, either.

For a start, it was the size of a horse!

Sinbad thought back to all those afternoons he'd spent reading travellers' tales in his father's library. He remembered that an Italian called Marco Polo had made it all the way to China and back. He claimed to have seen a bird called the Roc that was as large as a mountain, and big enough to carry away a fully-grown elephant!

Maybe this was one of its eggs.

'At last!' thought Sinbad. He ran his hands across the smooth, warm shell and smiled. 'I have the makings of an adventure in front of me!'

Chapter 3

Then night fell, which was odd, because it fell very early, very quickly and with the sound of great beating wings.

Sinbad looked up. 'That's not night falling!' he cried. 'Help!'

Above him, a colossal bird – so fantastically big that her body filled the sky and blocked out the sun – was swooping down towards him.

'A Roc!' gasped Sinbad. 'Just like Marco Polo saw! Oh my goodness! She's coming back to sit on her egg!'

In a split second, he flattened himself against the jagged cliff face. Any later and he would have been crushed by the Roc's tree-sized legs as they slammed down onto the ground.

'What am I going to do now?' thought Sinbad as the Roc snuggled down onto her egg. 'Don't panic, that's the important thing. Heroes are resourceful. When they find themselves in tight spots, they think up clever ways to get out of them.'

So Sinbad thought and thought until at last he had an idea. He undid his turban and used it to tie himself to one of the Roc's massive legs.

Sure enough, the next morning, when the Roc flew off in search of food, she took Sinbad with her!

It was very exciting.

At first.

'Yippee!' cried Sinbad as the mother Roc flew higher and higher. This was an adventure all right, and, with any luck, she might even carry him off the island.

Fat chance.

The Roc just kept going straight up, through the clouds and on, until Sinbad began to worry that she was taking him all the way to the moon! He clung onto her legs as tightly as he could, but the higher they went, the colder he felt, and soon his hands were like two blocks of ice.

'G-g-go b-b-back d-d-down! P-p-please!'
Sinbad begged through chattering teeth. Perhaps
the Roc heard him, for quite suddenly she
changed direction and went plunging down
towards the earth. Sinbad's stomach turned
cartwheels. He prayed he wouldn't be sick: at the
speed and direction he was travelling, it would
end up all over him.

'Nrrk!' was all he could say as they tore back
down through the clouds. They were going so
fast Sinbad was sure the Roc had lost control and
was about to crash. He shut his eyes, waited to be
smashed to bits and just hoped it wouldn't hurt
too much.

It didn't hurt at all.

'Can it be?' thought Sinbad. 'We didn't crash
after all! It's a miracle! Hooray!'

Then he opened his eyes.

About ten metres away from him, a gigantic
serpent – with a head the size of a fat rhinoceros
– opened its vast, venom-stained mouth and
lunged at him.

Sinbad immediately did what any true hero would do in that situation. He screamed like a big, frightened baby.

'AAAAAAAAAAAAARRRRRRRGGGH!'

If he thought it would stop the serpent from eating him, he was wrong.

What *did* stop the serpent from eating him was what happened next. The Roc grabbed its head in her great beak and crushed it with a single bite.

The serpent's body went limp. Like a blackbird with an earthworm, only a lot bigger and a lot, *lot* scarier: the Roc had found her breakfast.

'*Okay*,' thought Sinbad. 'I think I've had enough excitement for one day.'

He untied his turban from the Roc's leg and jumped off just as the great bird beat her gigantic wings and took to the air.

Sinbad looked around.

He was down at the bottom of a valley that seemed to be full of ice.

'Ice?' thought Sinbad. 'Surely it's too hot for that!'

When he looked closer, he saw that it wasn't ice. The valley floor was covered with diamonds!

'It's just like the story books! I've made my fortune! I'm rich!' thought Sinbad as he stuffed his bag and pockets with the sparkling jewels. 'I've had a few sticky moments, but this is shaping up to be a rather good adventure after all!'

Then his heart sank: he still needed to find his way out of the valley and its sides were impossibly steep and high.

He spent hours trying to clamber up them, but each time he lost his footing and came tumbling back down to the valley floor.

'This is hopeless,' he cried.

Exhaustion and despair descended upon him and he sank down onto a rock and fell asleep.

Chapter 4

THWUNK!

Sinbad was woken by the sound of something large and wet hitting the ground next to him.

It was a joint of meat: big and raw and bloody.

'Where on earth did that come from?' Sinbad wondered and he looked up.

At the very top of the valley, high, high above him, he could just make out the tiny figures of men. Sure enough, they threw another joint of meat down to the valley floor.

THWUNK!

'I thought I was all alone on this island,' thought Sinbad. 'What are they doing here?'

His answer came when a giant Roc swooped down and picked up the joint with its great talons. As it soared off with its prize, Sinbad noticed something glittering on the underside of the meat.

Diamonds!

'Clever souls!' he cried. The men must be enterprising merchants! They wanted the diamonds but knew there was no way they could carry them out of the steep-sided valley themselves. Instead, they threw the joints of meat down so that the diamonds would stick into them. Then all the men had to do was wait for a Roc to pick up the meat and fly off with it to its nest. They'd go to the nest, scare the great bird away and take the diamonds.

What a brilliant idea!

It gave Sinbad an even better one.

The next time a Roc grabbed hold of a joint of meat, he was waiting for it. He jumped onto one of its great feet and tied himself to its leg.

The Roc carried Sinbad up out of that valley of death and diamonds and off to its nest.

Sure enough, the moment the Roc landed, a band of men huddled on a nearby ledge started shouting and screaming. In no time, they had put the Roc to flight. When they clambered across to collect their diamonds, they were a little surprised to see Sinbad standing there.

Especially when they recognised him.

'If it isn't my old shipmates!' cried Sinbad cheerfully. 'I knew you'd come and find me somehow. You would never be so heartless as to actually leave me behind on an island in the middle of nowhere! It was just a practical joke, wasn't it?'

'Erm …' said the merchants awkwardly, 'Yes.'

'Of course it was!' Sinbad continued. 'Anything else would be a *bad sin*, eh?'

He laughed and the merchants joined in warily.

'I'm so pleased you've developed a taste for pranks!' said Sinbad. 'I'm looking forward to playing lots and lots of them on you all during our voyage home.'

'We'd love to have you back on our ship, of course we would, but …' began one of the merchants.

'Don't worry, I can pay,' said Sinbad, and he reached into his bag and brought out a large handful of diamonds. The merchants licked their lips greedily. 'I'll buy your ship from you if need be. This time, though, I don't think we'll be stopping off at any islands, do you?'

The Feathers in the Flames

A story based on the Ancient Egyptian myth of Osiris

Chapter 1

 It was Kai's tree, and it had been for as long as he could remember.

All the animals and birds seemed to know as much. He never once saw any of them go near it. So you can imagine his surprise when he was climbing it late one afternoon and heard something moving about in the branches high above his head.

He scrambled up to the very top as quickly as he could. There he found a long, thin, dignified-looking grey heron.

'What do you think you're doing?' said Kai.

'I should have thought that was obvious,' the bird replied. With a flick of its long head it indicated a nest that it had nearly finished building.

'But this is my tree!' Kai protested.

The bird gave a short, squawking laugh.

'This tree has belonged to me since the beginning of time,' it declared. 'Before then, even, I should think. I can't be certain. At my age, the memory starts to play tricks on you.'

'Since the beginning of time?' said Kai. 'This tree isn't that old!'

'It doesn't *look* that old, you mean,' said the bird. 'That is because it is a sacred tree, with magic in its rings. Why do you think no other bird or animal ever comes near it?'

'Because ... I thought ...' Kai stopped. Suddenly, he didn't know what he thought.

'Every thousand years or so, I hear it calling to me from across the world,' the bird went on. 'Everything else may change but this one tree remains exactly as it always was. So here I come to build my nest of cinnamon wood and wait.'

'What for?' asked Kai.

'Why the fire, of course!' said the bird. 'The fire that will burn me up into ashes so that out of the ashes a new bird can be born. That new bird will then carry what's left of me to Heliopolis so that I may be reunited with Re, the god of the sun.'

'Are you telling me you're the Phoenix?' said Kai.

'I am He Who Created Himself,' cried the bird, spreading its wings magnificently against the sinking sun. 'I am the sacred bird of Atum, of Re, of Osiris. I am the Bennu bird of Egypt, but, yes, some people do call me the Phoenix.'

'The Phoenix doesn't really exist,' said Kai. 'It's just an old legend.'

'Then you must be seeing things,' said the

- *Heliopolis:* (say) 'hee-lee-op-uh-liss'. • *Re:* (say) 'ray'.
  • *Atum:* (say) 'ah-toom'. • *Bennu:* (say) 'ben-oo'.

Bennu bird, 'because here I am. Hearing things too: did you ever meet another bird that could talk?'

'They tell me the yellowhammer says "a little bit of bread and no cheese," though I've never heard it,' said Kai. 'And you can teach my grandma's parrot to say all kinds of rude words, but it takes *hours*. I suppose you must be some kind of magical bird after all.'

'You are very kind,' said the Bennu bird. 'Now will you please leave me alone? After a thousand years in this body, I am very tired and I'd like to die.'

'But you're the wrong colour!' said Kai. 'The Phoenix has red and gold feathers. It lives for five hundred years, not a thousand!'

'The Egyptians say one thing about

me, the Greeks another,' said the Bennu bird. 'The Chinese say something else again, and you know what? I have lived so many lives since the god Atum made the world that they are *all* true. Sometimes I am a heron, sometimes a stork. Sometimes I am the red and gold firebird. I have been a man with the head of a bird, I have been a bird with the head of a man, but I have always been myself.'

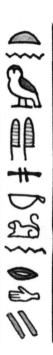

'So what was it like at the beginning of time?' asked Kai.

'A lot quieter than this!' snapped the bird. Kai showed no sign of leaving, so it sighed and settled itself.

In a faraway voice it said, 'The first thing I remember is

flying over water. I was a yellow wagtail then: Atum's bird. Water covered the face of the earth. It shone in the sun like mother of pearl. Then all at once, I saw a single rock sticking up out of that worldwide sea. I was so tired, I landed on it to rest my poor wings and I gave a great cry. That cry broke the silence of forever and so time began.'

'You began time?' said Kai.

'Time', said the Bennu bird, 'is the third most important gift I gave to mankind.'

'Only the third?' said Kai. 'If time hadn't got started, I would never have been born, and that would have been a *disaster*!'

'Hmmm,' said the bird, sounding unconvinced. 'You don't think the sunrise is more important?'

'That was you too?' asked Kai.

'When I was the Ba of Re,' nodded the bird. 'A Ba is like a god's soul, only it lives outside his body. Back then I wore my red and gold feathers, and my crown was the great disc of the sun itself.

'Every morning I would rise up with Re into the sky and shine light upon the world. Then, when it grew late, I would travel in his boat down into the Land of the Dead, and leave mankind to darkness and the night.'

The bird shivered.

'What is it like, the Land of the Dead?' asked Kai.

'I didn't linger there,' said the bird. 'I couldn't. In no time, we had to leave again and start a new day.'

'But the sun seems to rise every day without you now,' said Kai.

'Does it?' said the bird. 'I suppose it's got the hang of it and doesn't need reminding. Though it was going down to the Land of the Dead – and coming back out again – that gave me the idea for the most important gift of all.'

'More important than time?' said Kai. 'More important than the sunrise?'

'People can live without clocks,' said the bird. 'They can live without sunlight even, if they have to. What they cannot live without is hope. Do you know the story of Osiris?'

'No,' said Kai.

'I do sometimes wonder what they're teaching in the schools these days,' said the bird. 'It's certainly not manners. All right then, I have enough energy for one more story. If I tell you the tale of Osiris and my greatest gift, do you promise to leave me alone and let me die?'

'Do you have to die?' asked Kai.

'Do you also promise to stop asking silly questions?' snapped the bird.

'I promise,' said Kai reluctantly.

Chapter 2

'Osiris was a god,' began the bird, 'and a magnificent-looking one at that. He wore beautiful robes, a great crown and his skin was bright green.'

'Green?' said Kai.

'Osiris was the god of nature,' said the bird. 'With his queen, Isis, he reigned over the turning of the seasons. He made sure the river Nile would flood so that the land would be fertile. It was thanks to him that the crops grew and the people were fed.

'Now Osiris was a good soul; he was charming and friendly and kind. You might think that someone like that is bound to have a happy life, but being blessed with such a sunny outlook can be a curse. For, having no darkness in his heart, Osiris was unable to see any shadow in the hearts of others.

'Osiris had a younger brother called Set. He was the god of chaos, of the desert and of

the Land of the Dead – he was *all* shadow. Set hated Osiris and longed to kill him. In time, he planned the perfect way to finish off his poor, unsuspecting brother.

'Set threw a party for all the gods. Once
everyone was in a good mood, he brought out
a coffin.'

'A coffin?' said Kai.

'No one thought there was anything odd
about it,' said the bird. 'Not even when Set said,
"Whoever fits into this coffin, I shall give it to
him as a gift"!'

'Strange gift,' said Kai.

'The other gods tried it,' said the bird, 'but
they were all too tall or too fat, because Set had
made sure that it would only fit Osiris.'

'He didn't get into the coffin, did he?' asked Kai.

'As I have told you,' said the bird, 'Osiris thought everyone else was as happy and kind as he.'

'He was stupid, you mean!' said Kai.

'He was *good*,' the bird corrected him sternly. 'He saw no reason not to trust his brother and he climbed into the coffin. "How is it in there?" Set asked, once Osiris had got nice and comfy.

'"A perfect fit!" declared Osiris and everyone at the party cheered!

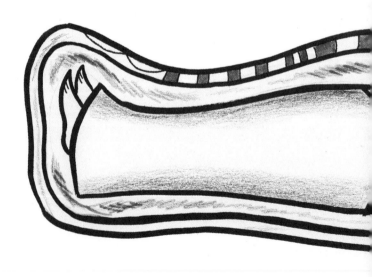

'At once, Set slammed the lid shut, locked it and sealed it with lead. Then, with the help of his wicked henchmen, he threw the coffin into the Nile!

'As you can imagine, there was uproar at the party: screaming and wailing and tables going over and waiters running about like headless chickens and no one knowing what to do. By the time everyone had calmed down, it was too late. The Nile had carried that coffin far, far away.

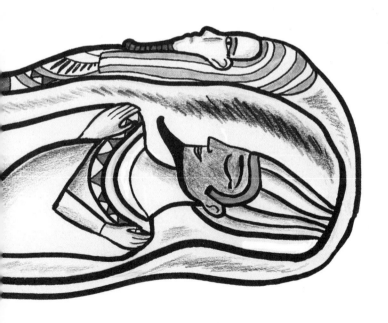

Chapter 3

'This story has a terrible villain, but it also has a hero – or a heroine, I should say – and that is Isis, Osiris' queen. She looked everywhere for that coffin. She never gave up the hope that she would find Osiris again.

'Finally, word came to her that the coffin had turned up in a place called Byblos. Isis went straight there. It was complicated, because the coffin had somehow got embedded in the trunk of a cedar tree. That would have been fine, but the King of Byblos had used that cedar tree as a column to hold up the roof of his new palace.

'Now the King of Byblos didn't want anybody, goddess or not, ruining his palace. So, Isis was allowed to take the coffin from the cedar tree, *provided she swore not to damage anything*!

'"What a nerve!" is what I would have said!' snorted the bird. 'Though Isis was gracious even then. She managed to get the coffin without bringing the palace down on the head of that foolish king – though that would have been no more than he deserved!'

The bird took a deep breath, then continued: 'Isis opened the coffin, and there was her dear husband Osiris, dead: drowned by the waters of the Nile. Isis sat by the coffin for days, until she had almost wept herself a new Nile. When at last her eyes ran dry, she found a beautiful spot in the desert and she buried him.'

'The desert!' said Kai. 'But I thought you said Set was the god of the desert!'

'You're not as stupid as you look, are you?' said the bird.

Kai wasn't sure if that was a compliment.

'Of course,' the bird went on before Kai could think too much about it, 'Set, being the god of the desert, knew all about it and the moment Isis left Osiris' grave, he dug the poor fellow up again! This time, he cut his body into twelve pieces – one for each month of the year. Then he scattered the pieces all over Egypt so that the crocodiles would get them and no one could ever put Osiris back together again.

'This made things rather awkward because Osiris was supposed to father a new god, called Horus. He hadn't got round to it by the time Set killed him.'

'So what happened?' asked Kai.

'Isis!' said the bird. 'Just as before, she searched all over the place until she found every last piece of her husband's body. Then she put them all back together again.'

'But he was dead,' said Kai. 'He wasn't going to be fathering any gods in that state, was he?'

'Ah, but Isis had an idea, a world-changing idea!' roared the Bennu bird. 'Where did she get

91

that idea from? Let's just say a little bird told her.'

'You mean you –' Kai started.

'I had been down into the Land of the Dead, don't forget,' said the bird. 'And I had come back out of it again with the reborn sun. As the crops sprout anew after the dead months of winter, as the tree dresses its bare branches with fresh leaves in the warmth of every spring, so I gave Isis the promise of new life. I gave her hope.'

'Wow,' said Kai.

'Sure enough,' said the bird, 'with hope in her heart, Isis sang a sacred song and Osiris came back to her, and, in time, Horus was born!'

'You mean Osiris rose again from the dead?' asked Kai.

The bird did not answer immediately. The effort of telling the story had tired it and it suddenly seemed very old.

'For a little while he did,' it murmured. It blinked its dimming eyes and bowed its heavy head. 'Then he had to return to the Land of the Dead, where he became lord in place of his

wicked brother Set. His time had come, you see, and none of us can escape when it is our time. No, no.'

Kai opened his mouth to ask another question, but the Bennu bird's eyes closed. At once the dry wood of its nest burst into flames.

'Not yet!' cried Kai. 'Wait! Please! There is so much more I want to know!'

He tried to reach into the fire, to grab the bird, but it was far too hot and all he did was singe his fingertips.

'Ouch!'

So Kai just sat and watched and sucked his fingers, until there was nothing left of that magnificent bird but a pile of ashes.

He waited for a long time for something to happen, but nothing did.

Night fell and Kai shivered in the cold.

'Perhaps there won't be another Phoenix after all,' Kai thought. 'Everything comes to an end eventually. Even I shall some day.'

The sweet-smelling cinnamon smoke must

have got into his eyes, for he felt them prickle.
A tear rolled down his cheek.

Then all at once he saw it. Deep in the heart
of that pile of ashes, something was stirring,
newly born.